MW00883981

Fariborz Lachini
Scent of Yesterday 1
Piano Sheet Music

Lachini Media – Canada
http://www.lachini.com

About Fariborz Lachini / Scent of Yesterday

Born in Iran, Lachini's musical career has spanned four decades and transcended both genres and borders - his musical sensibilities reflect a fusion of Persian and European styles, and the popularity and appeal of his music has expanded beyond the confines of his home country.

Scent of Yesterday is a collection of classic Persian Pop or folk melodies arranged for solo piano by composer/pianist Fariborz Lachini. Arrangements are in slower pace than the original pieces which makes the series an excellent choice for background music as well as instructional purposes but more so Lachini tries to bring back and reconstruct some of the best but almost forgotten melodies of his home country in his Scent of Yesterday series to a style enjoyable by today's audience. This is the companion sheet music book to his "Scent of Yesterday 1" album.

Music Arranged/Composed and Performed by
    Fariborz Lachini
    Lachini Media, Canada
    http://www.lachini.com

Music Engraved by
    David Shenton
    NY Music Publishing, USA
    http://shentonmusic.com

ISBN-13: 9-78-1441436481
ISBN-10: 1441436480

ISMN: 979-0-706060-07-1
UPC: 859701265092 / Scent of Yesterday 1 CD

Jane Maryam (Nazanine Maryam)

Kambiz Mozhdehi

Arranged by
Fariborz Lachini

Allegretto grazioso (♩ = 88)

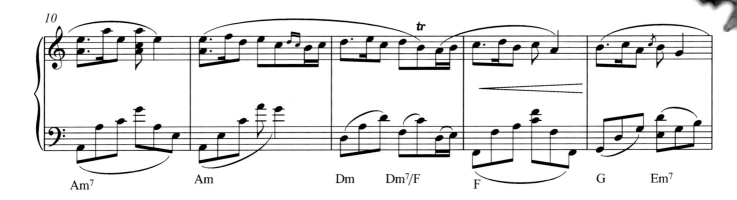

Jane Maryam

Jane Maryam

Jane Maryam

Jane Maryam

6

Jane Maryam

Gole Goldoon

Fariborz Lachini

Andante con moto ($\quad$ = c. 90)

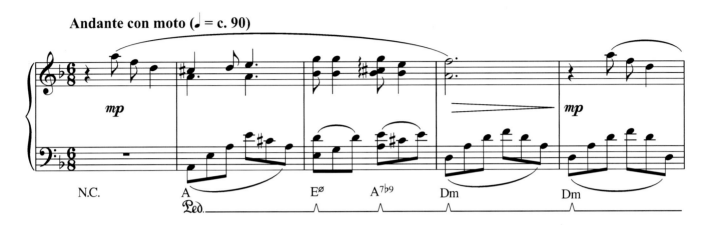

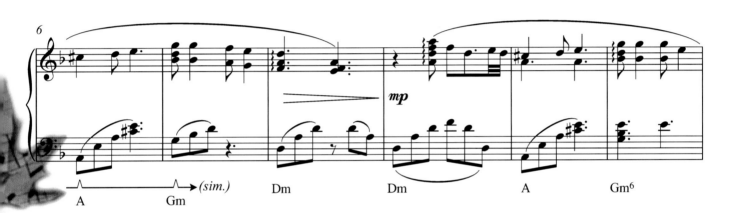

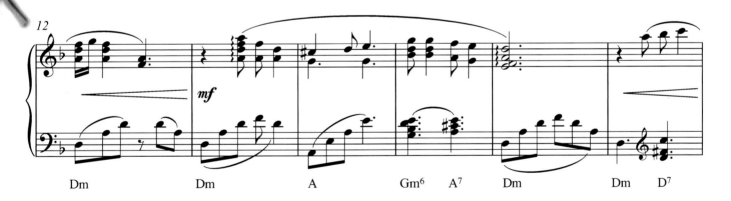

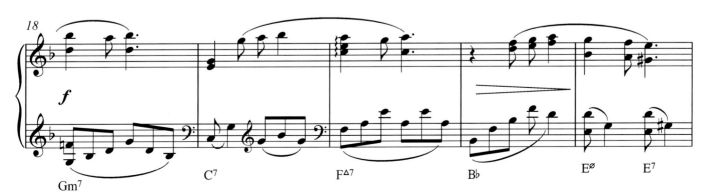

       Gole Goldoon

8

Gole Goldoon

Gole Goldoon

Ayeneha

Hassan Shamaizadeh

Arranged by
Fariborz Lachini

Andantino teneramente (♩ = 88)

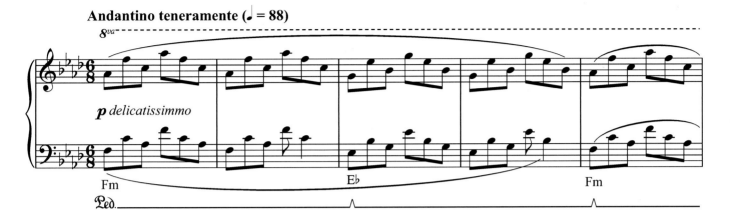

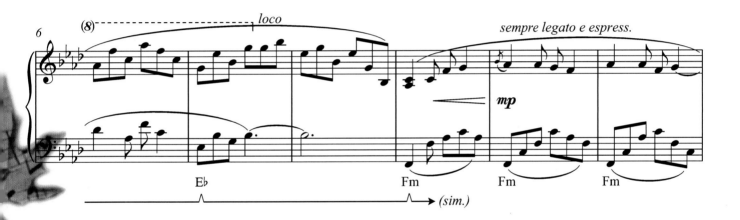

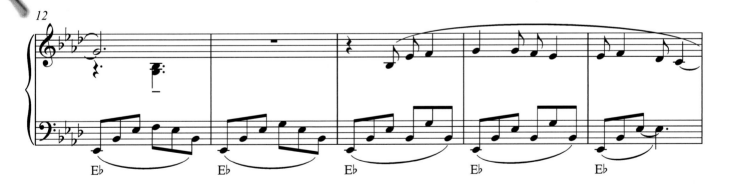

Ayeneha

Ayeneha

Ayeneha

Ayeneha

Ayeneha

Ayeneha

Ghoghaye Setaregan

Homayoon Khorram

Arranged by
Fariborz Lachini

Moderato e tranquillo (♩ = 72)

Ghoghaye Setaregan

Ghoghaye Setaregan

Ghoghaye Setaregan

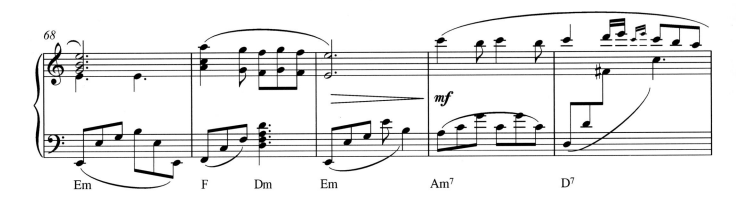

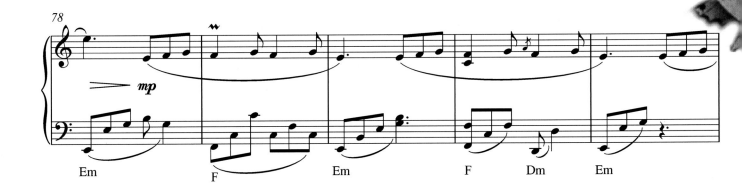

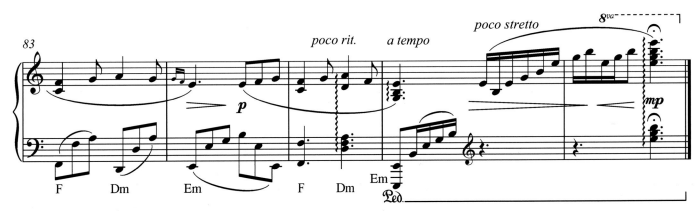

Ghoghaye Setaregan

Ayrilikh

Ali Seidi

Arranged by
Fariborz Lachini

Lento sostenuto (♩ = 60)

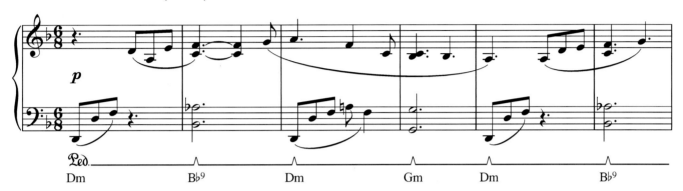

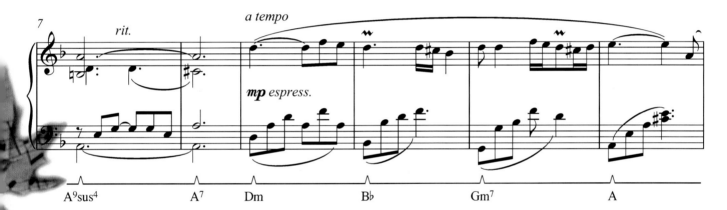

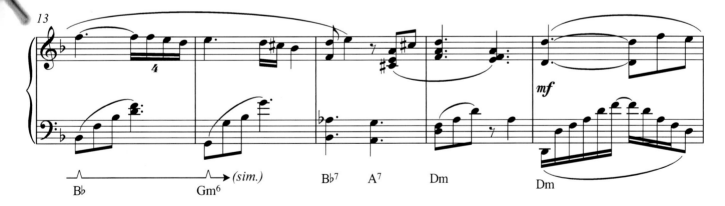

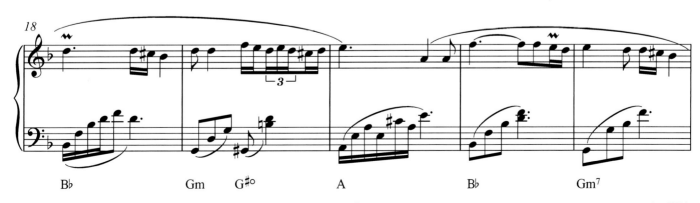

1 of 5

Ayrilikh

Ayrilikh

24

4 of 5

Ayrilikh

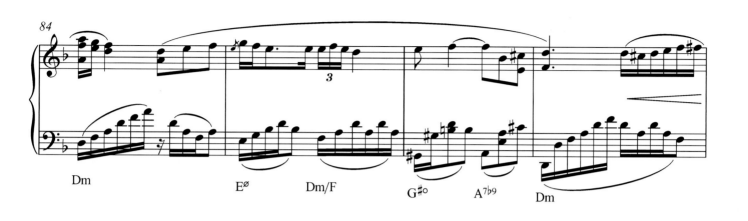

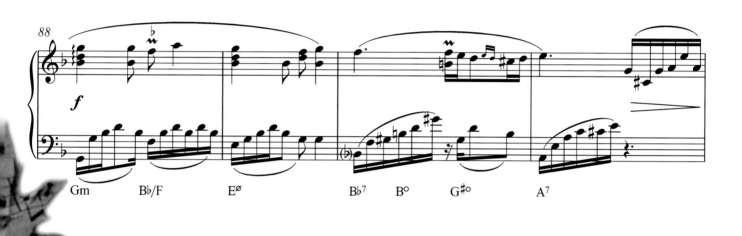

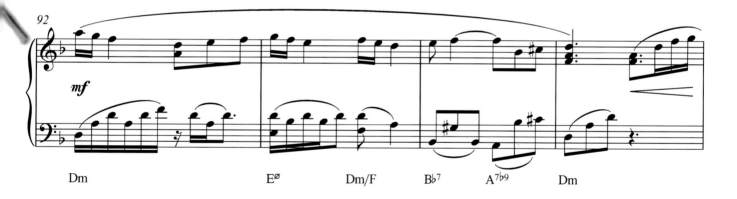

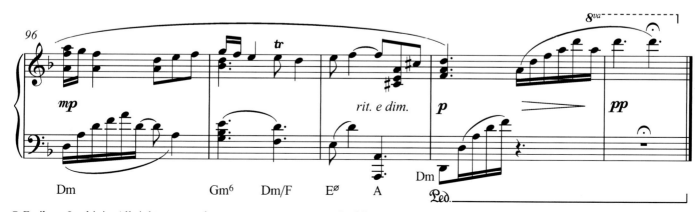

5 of 5

Ayrilikh

Ashegham Man

Anoushirvan Rohani

Arranged by
Fariborz Lachini

Ashegham Man

Ashegham Man

28

Ashegham Man

4 of 5

Ashegham Man

30

5 of 5

Ashegham Man

Cheshme Man

Hassan Shamaizadeh

Arranged by
Fariborz Lachini

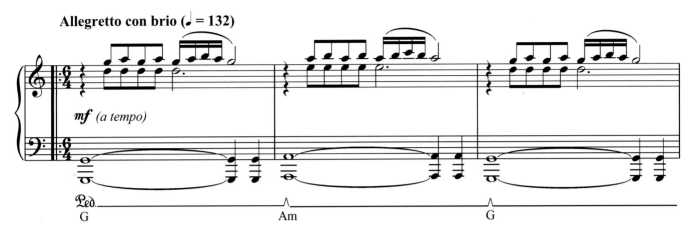

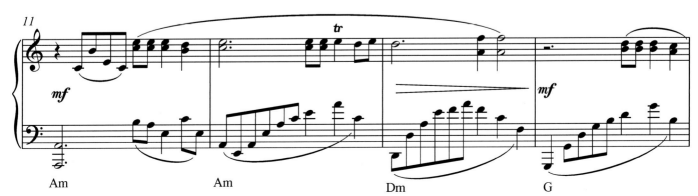

1 of 5

32

2 of 5

Cheshme Man

Cheshme Man

34

Cheshme Man

Cheshme Man

Khabam Ya Bidaram

Varouzhan

Arranged by
Fariborz Lachini

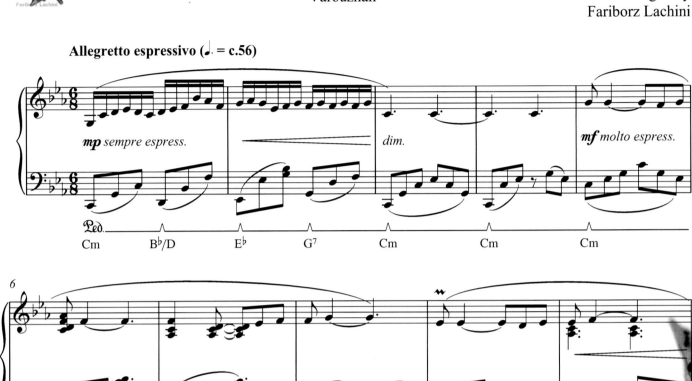

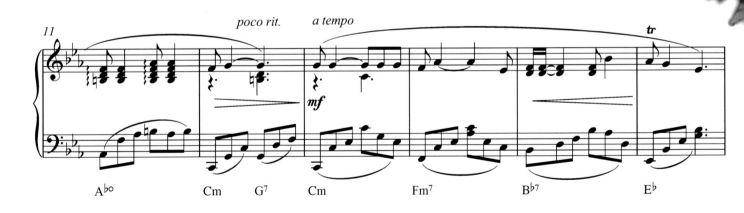

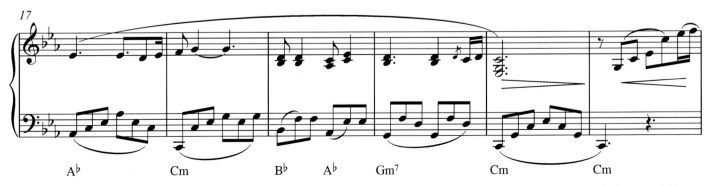

Khabam Ya Bidaram

Khabam Ya Bidaram

38

3 of 3

Khabam Ya Bidaram

Daghestan

Traditional Armenian

Arranged by
Fariborz Lachini

Daghestan

40

2 of 3

Daghestan

Daghestan

Age Ye Rooz

Faramarz Aslani

Arranged by
Fariborz Lachini

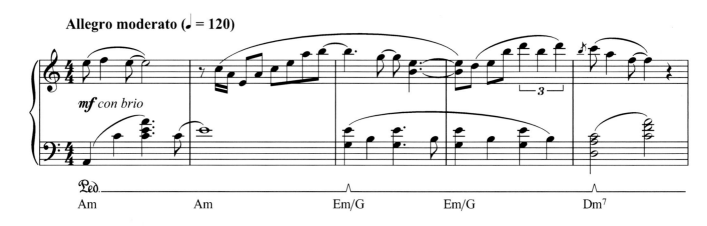

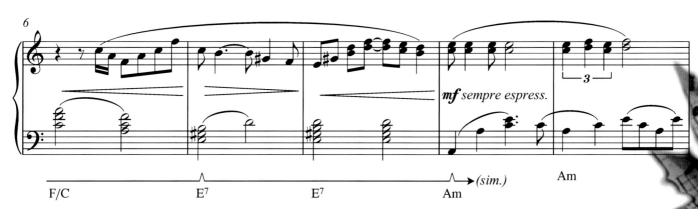

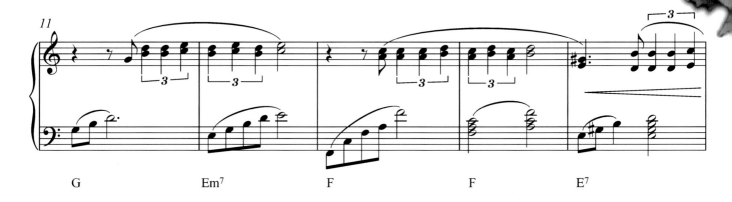

Age Ye Rooz

Age Ye Rooz

44

Age Ye Rooz

Age Ye Rooz

46

5 of 5

Age Ye Rooz

Bavar Kon

Varouzhan

Arranged by
Fariborz Lachini

Lento triste (♩ = 66)

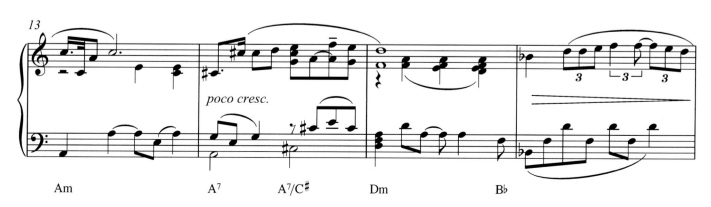

Bavar Kon

48

Bavar Kon

37
B⌀/A Am Am F° Am Am
41
Dm6 Dm6 B⌀ B⌀ E7♭9
45
Am B7 E7♭9 Am E7 Am
49
cresc.
f
G° A7 Dm Dm/C B♭ Am
53
mf
cresc.
B7/A E7+ Am A G° Dm

© Fariborz Lachini - All rights reserved

50

Bavar Kon

Eshghe To Nemimireh

Shahram Zandi

Arranged by
Fariborz Lachini

Eshghe To Nemimireh

Eshghe To Nemimireh

Eshghe To Nemimireh

Eshghe To Nemimireh

Gahvareh

Varouzhan

Arranged by
Fariborz Lachini

Andante sostenuto ($\bullet$ = c.48)

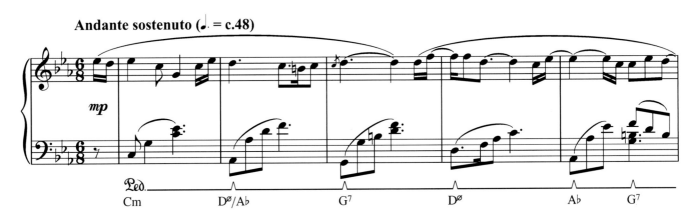

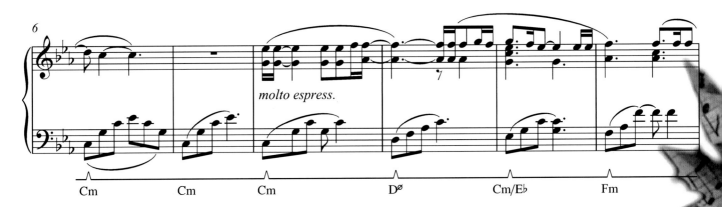

1 of 4   Gahvareh

57

2 of 4

Gahvareh

Gahvareh

Gahvareh

Gole Sorkh

Homayoon Khorram

Arranged by
Fariborz Lachini

Gole Sorkh

61

2 of 5

Gole Sorkh

Gole Sorkh

Gole Sorkh

Gole Sorkh

Lalayee

Varouzhan

Arranged by
Fariborz Lachini

Lalayee

Lalayee

Lalayee

4 of 4

Lalayee

Made in the USA
Las Vegas, NV
03 November 2024

11052844R00043